I0816479

AMAZING OCEAN LIFE

Stingrays

by Colleen Sexton

Kaleidoscope
Minneapolis, MN

Where the Quest for Discovery Begins

This edition first published in 2023 by Kaleidoscope Publishing, Inc.

Kaleidoscope Publishing, Inc.
6012 Blue Circle Drive
Minnetonka, MN 55343

Library of Congress Control Number
2022937429

ISBN
978-1-64519-567-2 (library bound)
978-1-64519-637-2 (ebook)

Bigfoot Jr. lurks within one of the images in this book. It's up to you to find him!

Table of Contents

By the Seashore 4
Flat Fish 8
Crushing It 14
Hide and Sting 18
Photo Glossary 22
Read More 23
Index 24
About the Author 24

By the Seashore

Waves wash over a stingray. It is hiding on the sea floor.

Stingrays are **fish**. They live in oceans around the world.

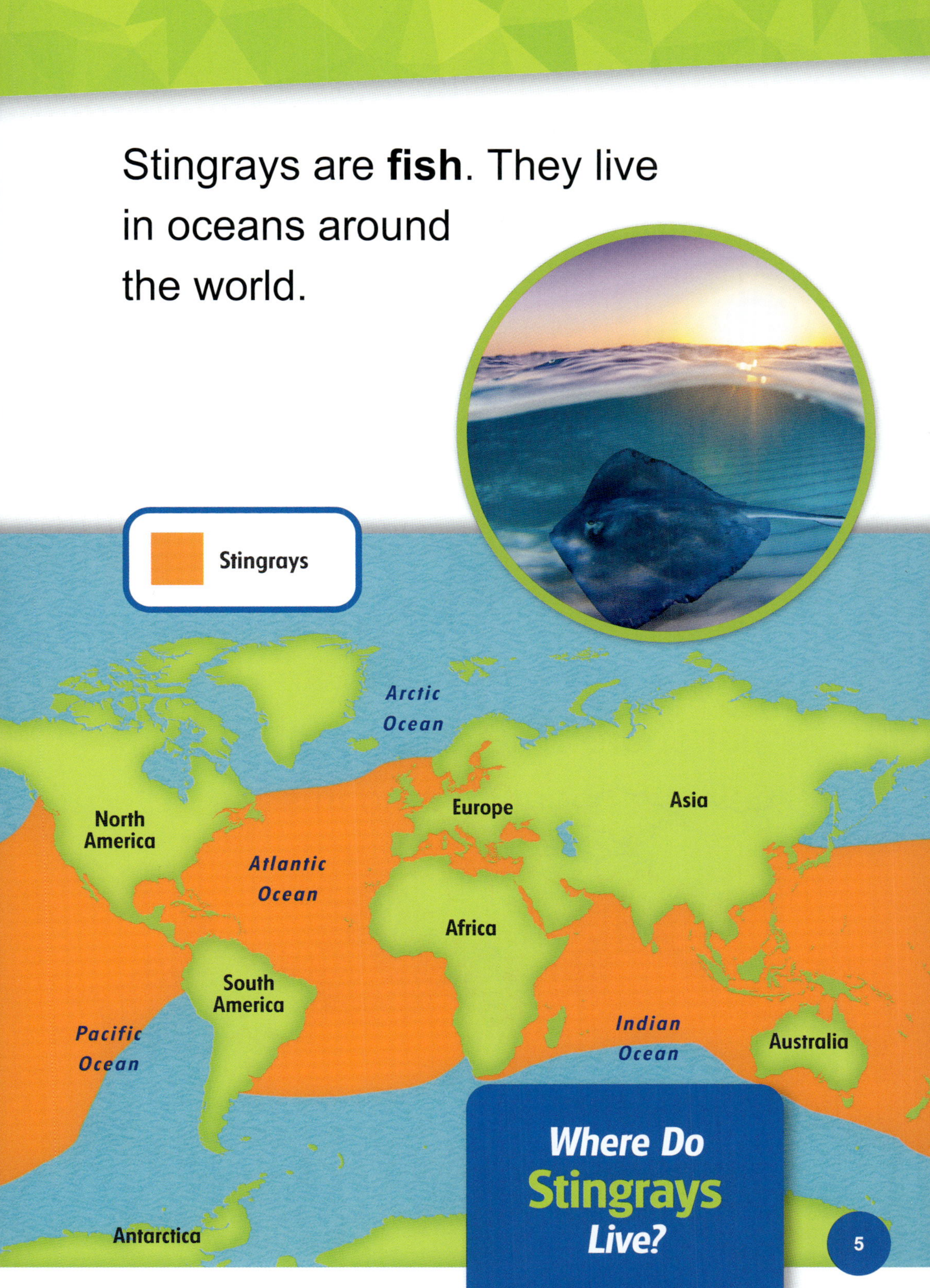

Where Do Stingrays Live?

Stingrays are found in warm water near shore. They spend most of their lives partly buried in sand.

There are more than 200 kinds of stingrays.

The **tide** moves stingrays to deeper water and then back toward shore.

Flat Fish

A stingray's body is flat and wide. It does not have bones like other fish.

Its skeleton is made of rubbery **cartilage**. Cartilage helps the stingray bend its body.

FUN FACT
A stingray looks like it is smiling when seen from the bottom.

A stingray has eyes on top of its body. Its mouth and **nostrils** are on its underside.

A stingray breathes through **gills**.

A stingray flaps its wide **fins** up and down to swim. The stingray looks like a bird flying underwater!

A stingray has a long tail that looks like a whip. The tail has a sharp **spine**.

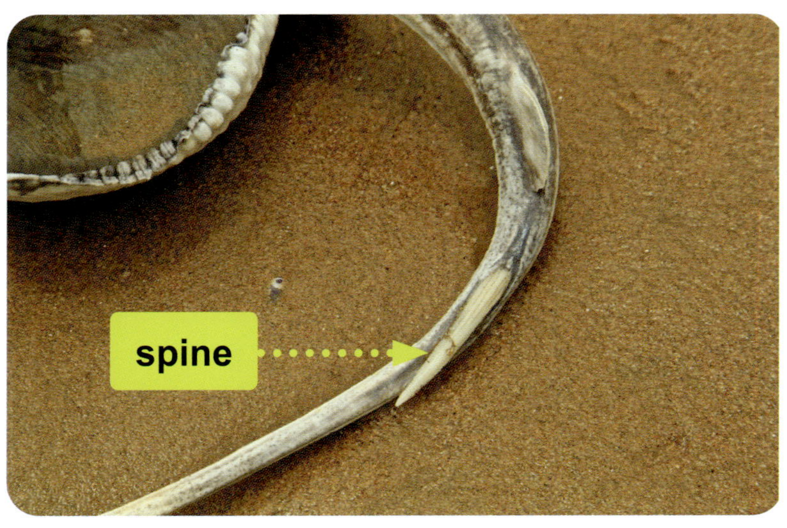

Some stingrays swim by moving their bodies like waves.

Parts of a Stingray

Crushing It

A stingray is hunting. It waits for **prey** on the sea floor.

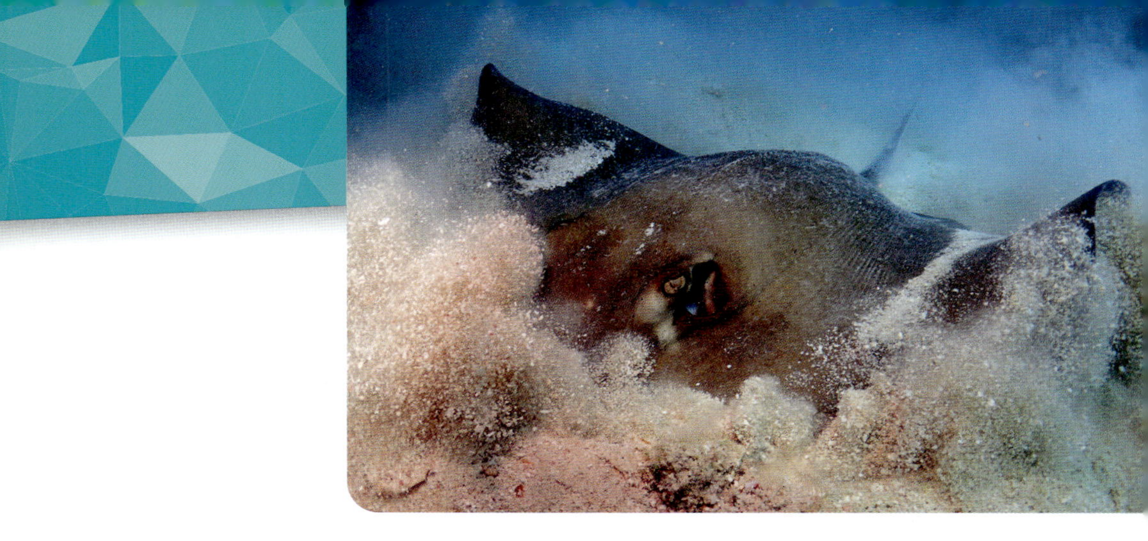

A clam moves in the sand. The stingray jumps on it!

What Do Stingrays Eat?

Slurp! The stingray sucks the clam into its mouth. Its strong jaws crush the clam's shell.

A stingray's teeth often break off when it eats. But new teeth always grow in.

The stingray chews and swallows the clam. It spits out the shell.

Hide and Sting

A stingray covers itself with sand to hide from **predators**.

FUN FACT
The top of a stingray's body has colors and patterns that match the sea floor.

But a shark finds the stingray. The stingray flaps its fins and swims away. It escapes!

What Eats Stingrays?

sharks

sea lions

seals

When a stingray cannot escape. It swings its tail to hit the shark.

The tail's sharp spine sends poison into the shark. *Ouch!* The shark stops and the stingray gets away!

Photo Glossary

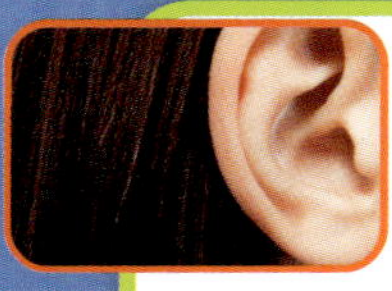

cartilage: A strong, bendable material. Cartilage helps the stingray bend its body.

fins: Flaps on a fish's body used for swimming. A stingray flaps its wide fins up and down to swim.

fish: A cold-blooded animal that lives in water and has gills, fins, and scales. Stingrays are fish.

gills: Slits near the mouth that a fish uses to breathe. The gills move oxygen from the water to the fish's blood.

nostrils: Openings in a body used for smelling. A stingrays nostrils are on its underside.

predator: An animal that hunts other animals for food. A stingray covers itself with sand to hide from predators.

prey: An animal that is hunted by another animal for food.A stingray waits on the sea floor for prey.

spine: A hard, sharp point on a stingray's tail. The spine in a stingray's tail sends poison into the shark.

tide: The rising and falling of the ocean twice each day. The tide moves stingrays to deeper water and then back toward the shore.

Read More

Leaf, Christina. *Stingrays.* Ocean Animals. Minneapolis, MN: Bellwether Media, 2021.

Terp, Gail. *Stingrays.* Super Sea Creatures. Mankato, MN: Black Rabbit Books, 2021.

Zommer, Yuval. *The Big Book of the Blue*. New York, NY: Thames & Hudson, 2018.

Websites

Factsurfer.com gives you a safe, fun way to find more information.

1. Go to www.factsurfer.com.
2. Enter "Stingrays" into the search box and click
3. Select your book cover to see a list of related websites.

About the Author

Colleen Sexton is a writer and editor. She is the author of more than one hundred nonfiction books for kids on topics ranging from astronauts to glaciers to elephants. She lives in Minnesota.

INDEX

body, 8, 9, 10, 18
fish, 5, 8
nostrils, 10, 13
predators, 18
shore, 6, 7
spine, 12, 13, 20

PHOTO CREDITS

The images in this book are reproduced through Shutterstock: Arunee Rodloy 3; Lauren Wang 4; Drew McArthur 5; Miroslav Halama 6; maya_parf 6; Nantawat Chotsuwan 6; Nataliya Hora 7; Durden Images 8; Vicki L. Miller 10; Madison Muskopf 11, 22; JINXI 12, 22; clayton harrison 12, 22; JIANG HONGYAN 13; MartinRejzek 14; DoublePHOTO studio 15; koosen 15; HP Productions 15; Kyle Lippenberger 15; Jiang Zhongyan 15; oksana2010 15; Glenn Price 15; Reimar 16; Andrea Izzotti 16; Vladimir Turkenich 17; Anita Kainrath 18; StudioSmart 19; Eric Isselee 20; Nerthuz 20; Siamdive 21; Dmitry Rukhlenko 22; diy13 22; Ninell 22; Stefan Pircher 22; Ruslan.Salikhov 22; Rich Carey 23. Cover: Ruslan.Salikhov, Pong471, Solarisys.